17 Prehistoric Beasts

Everyone Should Know About

Stanton F. Fink

Volume I of Stanton's Coloring books

Acknowledgments

and Dedication

To my father, in whose books I discovered my first monsters.

To Will Caligan, whose help and encouragement is one of the primary reasons for this coloring book's existence.

To Mariano Silvera, who should have had his own artbooks

To Doctor David Morafka, who helped teach me to be more picky with my information.

To my friends, who helped push me to make this.

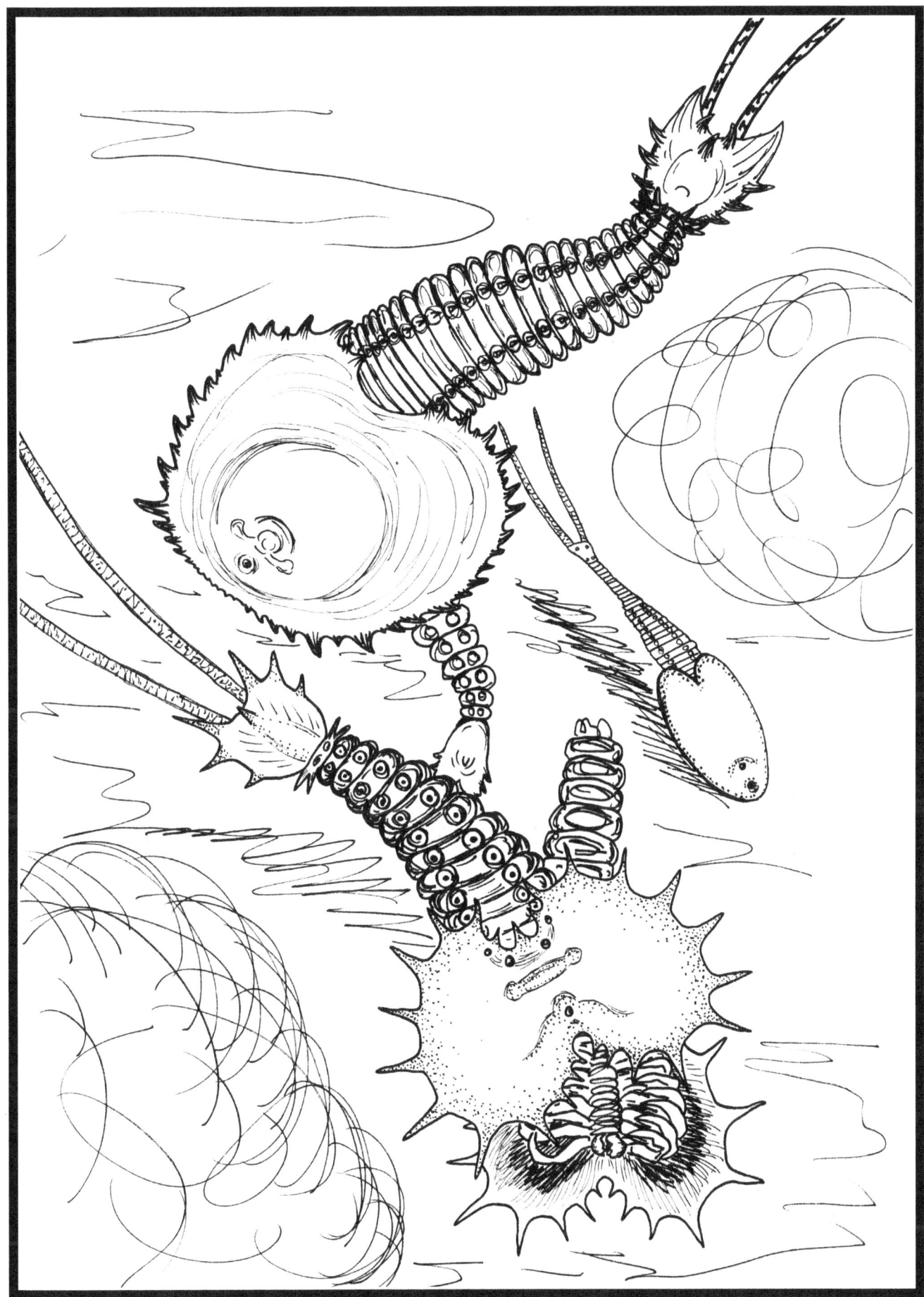

Table of Contents

Introduction

The purpose of this coloring book series is to provide information on various prehistoric animals both profoundly famous and incredibly obscure to artists of all ages. Of course, there is a lot of material to work with, as animals have been a major component of Earth's ecosystems for at least 670 million years.

For the sake of space and workability, each volume will contain 17 entries: ideally, one species for each geological time period, if possible. If you, or your inner and or outer child do not see your favorite prehistoric animal here, it may be eventually featured in another volume. Or, contact me to have it put into a later volume.

Glossary

- **Aquatic**- Living in water.
- **Arthropod**- Any member of the animal phylum Arthropoda, including trilobites, arachnids, crustaceans, insects, myriapods and their relatives. All arthropods have armor-like, jointed exoskeletons made of chitin-derived plates, sometimes reinforced with calcium carbonate, and jointed limbs.
- **Cambrian**- A period of time in the Paleozoic Era from 541 to 485 million years ago.
- **Carboniferous**- A period of time in the Paleozoic Era from 359 to 300 million years ago.
- **Cenozoic**- An era of time in the Phanerozoic Eon from 65 million years ago until now.
- **Chordate**- Any member of the animal phylum Chordata, including sea squirts, lancet fish, and vertebrates (such as lampreys, sharks, tuna, frogs, lizards, chickens, and people). All chordates have, at least at some point in their life cycle, a notochord, a long, flexible rod, usually made of cartilage, or, in the case of most vertebrates, cartilage and bone, running down the back from head to tail, directly beneath the neural tube.
- **Cnidarian**- Any member of the animal phylum Cnidaria, such as jellyfish, box jellies, Portuguese Man'o'war, sea anemones, coral and the parasitic myxozoans. Cnidarians are usually radially symmetrical, and have unique, venom-injecting stinging cells called "cnidocytes."
- **Cretaceous**- The last period of time in the Mesozoic Era, from 144 to 66 million years ago.
- **Devonian-** A period of time in the Paleozoic Era from 414 to 360 million years ago.
- **Ediacaran-** The last period of time in the Precambrian Eon from 635 to 542 million years ago.
- **Eocene-** A period of time in the Cenozoic Era from 55 to 33 million years ago.
- **Fauna-** In an ecological context, "fauna" refers to the animal components of an ecosystem.
- **Formation-** In a geological or paleontological context, a formation is a group of rock layers.
- **Gnathostome-** A gnathostome is any vertebrate chordate with a moveable jaw (or had an ancestor with one).
- **Holocene-** A period of time in the Cenozoic Era from 12,000 years ago until now.
- ***Incertae sedis*-** A Latin phrase literally meaning "uncertain seat." *"Incertae sedis"* is a term in classification used to refer to a species or group whose relationships with related organisms are unclear or poorly defined.
- **Jurassic-** The second period of time in the Mesozoic Era, from 199 to 145 million years ago.
- **Mesozoic-** An era of time in the Phanerozoic Eon from 249 to 66 million years ago.
- **Miocene-** A period of time in the Cenozoic Era from 23 to 5 million years ago.

- **Mollusk**- Any member of the animal phylum Mollusca, including snails, clams, squid, octopuses, tusk shells and chitons. Most mollusks have a calcium carbonate shell, and a toothed, file-like tongue called a radula. All mollusks have a cape-like organ, the mantle, which usually secretes the shell, and houses breathing organs, and a nervous system.
- **Nekton**- Any aquatic animal that lives either entirely or almost entirely in the water column, and relies on its own swimming or propulsion abilities to keep and move itself in and around the water column. Anchovies, porpoises and ichthyosaurs are examples of nekton.
- **Neogene**- The second third of the Cenozoic Era, comprising of the Miocene and the Pliocene periods.
- **Oligocene**- A period of time in the Cenozoic Era from 33 to 23 million years ago.
- **Ordovician**- A period of time in the Paleozoic Era from 484 to 440 million years ago.
- **Paleocene**- A period of time in the Cenozoic Era from 65 to 55 million years ago.
- **Paleogene**- The first third of the Cenozoic Era, comprising of the Paleocene, Eocene, and Oligocene.
- **Paleozoic**- An era of time in the Phanerozoic Eon from 249 to 66 million years ago.
- **Permian**- The last period of time in the Paleozoic Era, the time of "The Great Dying," or most severe of all known extinction events, from 299 to 250 million years ago.
- **Pharynx**- A structure in the throat of many animals located directly behind the mouth or oral chamber. In vertebrates, it often houses breathing structures, like gills.
- **Plankton**- An organism that uses water currents and waterflow to as its primary means of transportation in the water column because it is either too small to move long distances by its own power, or lacks the ability to propel itself entirely. Sargassum seaweed and jellyfish are two varieties of plankton.
- **Pleistocene**- A period of time in the Cenozoic Era from 3 million years ago until 12 thousand years ago.
- **Pliocene**- A period of time in the Cenozoic Era from 5 to 3 million years ago.
- **Quaternary**- The last third of the Cenozoic Era, comprising of the Pleistocene and the Holocene periods.
- **Terrestrial**- Living on land.
- **Triassic**- The first period of time in the Mesozoic Era, from 249 to 200 million years ago.

Name	Haoot
Species	*Haootia quadriformis*
Phylum	Cnidaria
Class	*incertae sedis*
Size	56 mm by 34 mm
Time Period	Late Ediacaran of the Precambrian, 560 million years ago
Location	Bonavista Peninsula, Newfoundland, Canada
Comments	The Haoot, *Haootia quadriformis*, is a Precambrian-aged, chalice-shaped animal from the Lost Point Fauna of what is now Newfoundland, Canada. Inhabitants of the Lost Point ecosystem lived in a marine environment deep enough underwater to lack access to sunlight. Local laws forbid extracting rocks or fossils from protected areas, so, the two known fossils are still in Bonavista Peninsula, though researchers made several casts of them to study.

The haoot is identified as a cnidarian polyp, and is one of the very few Precambrian animals whom researchers are actually confident about identifying its living relatives. Even so, even though the haoot is a cnidarian, researchers have been unable to determine which class it belongs in, or if it comes from a time in cnidarian evolution where the different cnidarian groups had yet to evolve and diversify yet.

The lifestyle is unknown: the haoot may have eaten plankton, or it may have absorbed dissolved nutrients directly from the water. It probably wasn't carnivorous, and definitely could not have used symbiotic algae to photosynthize with like modern coral or sea anemones.

Other members of the Lost Point Fauna include the candelabrum-like *Primocandelabrum*, the lozenge-shaped *Fractofusus,* the conical *Thectardis*, the lettuce-leaf-like *Bradgatia*, and the triangle-like *Triforillonia*.

Name	Magnifiworm
Species	*Yuyuanozoon magnificissimi*
Phylum	Chordata
Subphylum	Vetulicolia
Class	Vetulicolida
Family	Vetulicolidae
Size	20.2 centimeters
Time Period	"Stage 3" of the Cambrian Period, 515 million years ago
Location	Chengjiang County, Yunnan Province, China
Comments	The Magnifiworm, *Yuyuanozoon magnificissimi,* is the largest known chordate from the Cambrian, the only known fossil specimen measuring a whopping 20.2 centimeters long. Its fossil is from the Early Cambrian of Yunnan, China, as a member of the Chengjiang Fauna. The closest living relatives of the magnifiworm and other vetulicolians are the sea squirts. The magnifiworm swam around in the water column near the seafloor, and probably siphoned up edible particles as it sucked water into its pinhole mouth.

Although the fossil specimen is perfectly preserved (sort of, what with it being squashed flat), the magnifiworm's anatomy provides few clues about its lifestyle. When alive, the animal would have looked something like a segmented egg with a long, segmented tail. Because the tail was originally cylindrical, researchers cannot determine if the tail moved side to side or up and down.

Here the magnifiworm is shown swimming past various other Chengjiang Fauna animals.

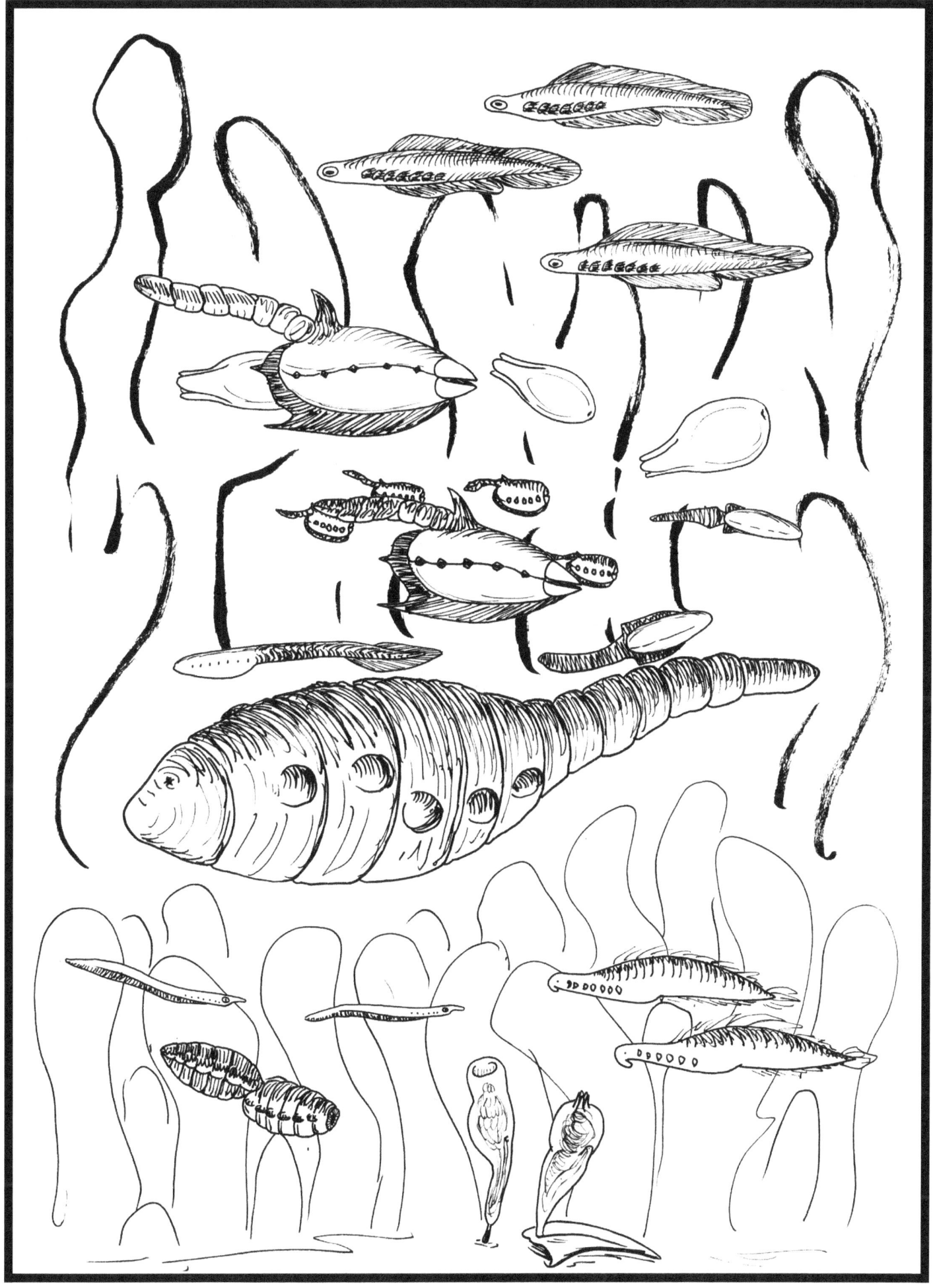

Name	Penteconter Sea Scorpion
Species	*Pentecopterus decorahensis*
Phylum	Arthropoda
Class	Merostomata
Order	Eurypterida
Family	Megalograptidae
Size	Somewhere between 1.7 meters and 1.83 meters
Time Period	Middle Ordovician, about 467 million years ago
Location	The Decorah Crater, Iowa, United States of America
Comments	The Penteconter Sea Scorpion is the oldest known sea scorpion, or eurypterid. Contrary to their name, sea scorpions are more closely related to horseshoe crabs, and were sometimes found in freshwater environments in addition to saltwater. "Penteconter" refers to a variety of ancient Greek warship, and is meant to describe the beast's presumed behavior of swimming about hither and yon in search of prey (probably other, smaller arthropods). The penteconter sea scorpion is also the third-largest eurypterid arthropod known, surpassed in size only by the bison-sized sea scorpion, *Acutiramus,* of Silurian Buffalo, New York, and the crocodile-sized freshwater sea scorpion, *Jaekelopterus,* which lived in rivers and estuaries of Germany and Wyoming during the early Devonian.

Name	Birkenfish
Species	*Birkenia elegans*
Phylum	Chordata
Class	Anaspida
Order	Birkeniida
Family	Birkeniidae
Size	Up to 10 centimeters in length
Time Period	Wenlock epoch of the Middle Silurian, 433 million years ago
Location	Great Britain and Norway
Comments	The Birkenfish, *Birkenia elegans,* is an anaspid jawless fish whose fossils are found in Middle to Late Silurian-aged marine strata of Great Britain and Norway. *B. elegans* lived in the water column of shallow-water marine environments along the coasts of the ancient continent of Laurentia. Although its mouth was beak-shaped, the birkenfish had no anatomical jaws, and could not move its mouth beyond widening and narrowing it via movement of its pharynx. As such, it probably ate plankton and very small animals that it sucked out of the water column through filter-feeding.

The name *Birkenia*, refers to Birkenhead Burn, a hill of great paleontological importance in Lanark County, Scotland. The species name, *"elegans,"* means slender, referring to the slender scales.

The big-headed organisms swimming with the birkenfish here are a species of extinct crustacean named *Ainiktozoon loganense*. The segmentation of the tail lead the first researchers to mistake it for myomeres or muscle units of a chordate.

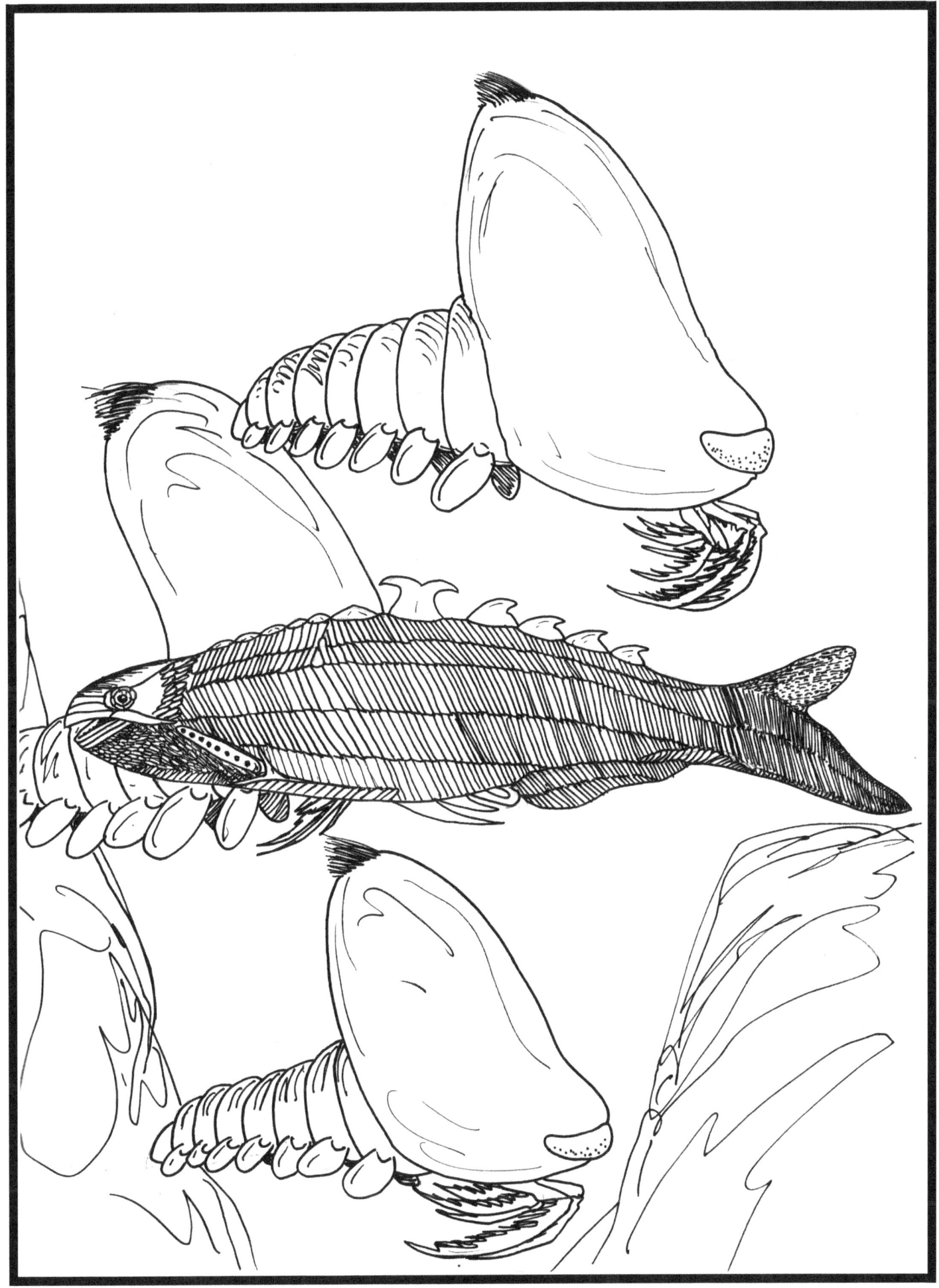

Name	Terrell's Terrorfish
Species	*Dunkleosteus terrelli*
Phylum	Chordata
Class	Placodermi
Order	Arthrodira
Family	Dunkleosteidae
Size	Estimated to be up to 6 meters in length
Time Period	Late Famennian epoch of the Late Devonian period, 360 to 358 million years ago
Location	Poland, Ohio, Pennsylvania, Tennessee, California and possibly Texas
Comments	Terrell's Terrorfish, named for Jay Terrell, the man who discovered the first specimens near Cleveland, Ohio, is one of the best known, if not the best known placoderm. Numerous fossils have been found in Late Devonian-aged shale in Ohio, and in other parts of the United States, as well as Poland.
	The terrorfish is thought to have swam in the water column and preyed on other large fish, probably including other placoderms, like *Gymnotrachelus*, *Titanichthys*, *Gorgonichthys*, *Selenosteus*, and *Dinichthys*. Prey was subdued with the terrorfish's bite, which researchers have calculated to have had the 2nd most powerful bite force among chordates, surpassed only by the bite of the giant shark, Megalodon.

Name	Tully's Monster
Species	*Tullimonstrum gregarium*
Phylum	? Chordata
Class	? Hyperoartia
Order	? Petromyzontiformes
Family	*incertae sedis*
Size	8 to 35 centimeters in length
Time Period	Middle Pennsylvanian epoch of the Carboniferous, about 300 million years ago
Location	Essex Biota of Mazon Creek, Grundy County, Illinois
Comments	Exactly what Tully's Monster, *Tullimonstrum gregarium* was, and where it belongs in the "tree of life" has vexed paleontologists ever since amateur fossil collect Francis Tully brought the first specimens to the Field Museum in Chicago in 1955.

Recent reexamination of fossils permitted researchers to better understand features, including cartilaginous rings, a notochord, and melanosomes in the eyes unique to vertebrate chordates, that lead them to deduce that this beast was either a (highly modified) lamprey, or a very close relative of lampreys.

Understanding Tully's monster's place in the fossil ecosystem, on the other hand, has been easier. The creature swam in the water column offshore of an estuary, using its modified tailfins to move and stabilize its body. Very small prey was located with its eyes, placed on eyestalks, and were seized and swallowed with its highly modified mouth at the end of a long, thin trunk.

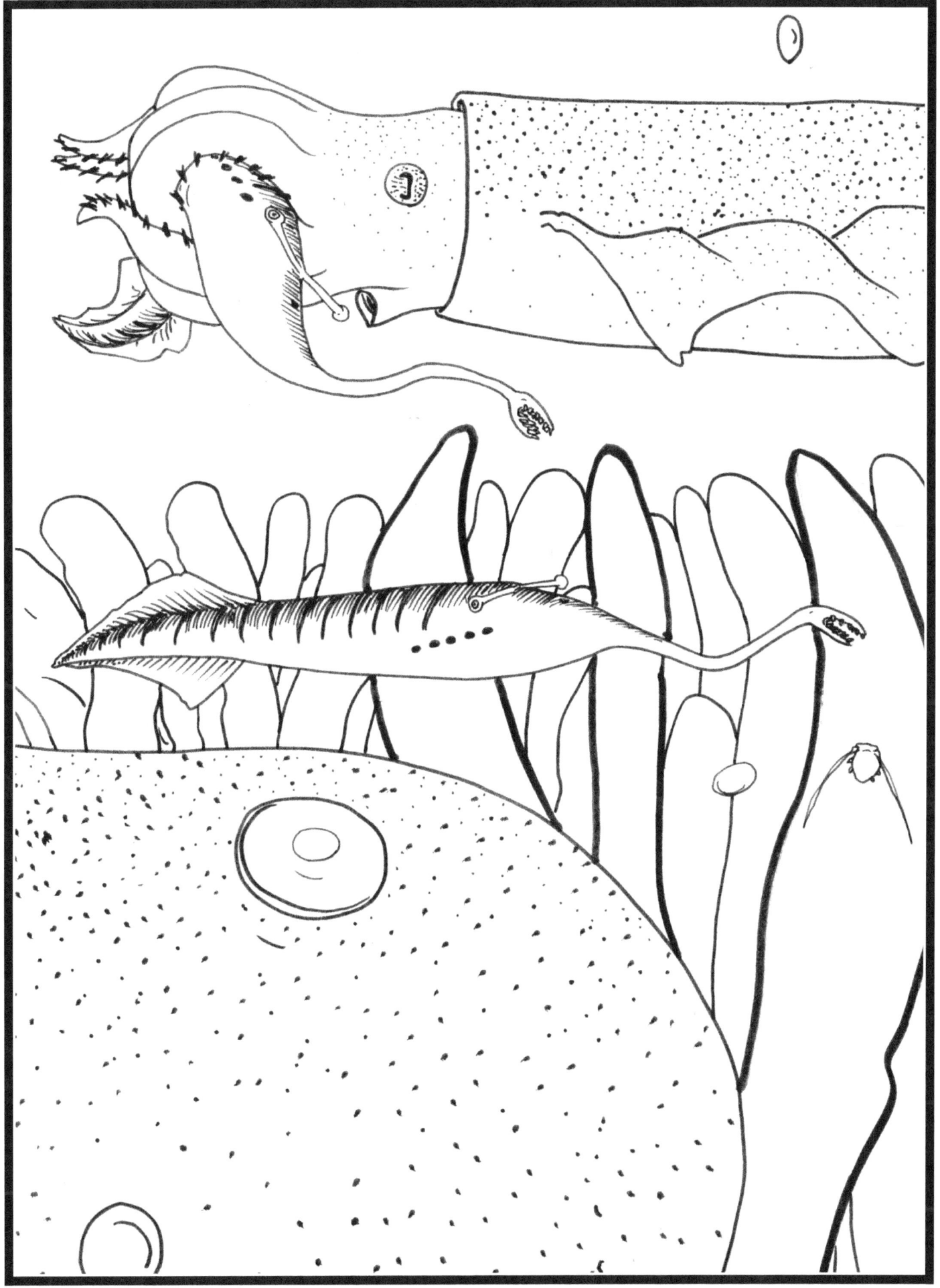

Name

Bonbon Proetid Trilobite

Species	*Triproetus bonbon*
Phylum	Arthropoda
Class	Trilobita
Order	Proetida
Family	Proetidae
Size	About 1 centimeter wide, and about 2 to 3 centimeters long
Time Period	From the Artinskian to Wordian epochs of the Middle Permian, about 283 to 267 million years ago
Location	Qarari Limestone of Wadi Khawr al Jaramah, Oman
Comments	The Bonbon Proetid Trilobite, *Triproetus bonbon,* lived in a somewhat shallow-water marine environment about 10 to 30 meters deep, filled with coral and brachiopods. The bonbon trilobite's fossils are beautifully well-preserved, leading scientists to suspect that the area either had very few water currents strong enough to damage or break apart the trilobites after death, or that the trilobites in the region were frequently killed by sudden burials, perhaps caused by underwater mudslides. Either way, *T. bonbon*'s fossils are so well-preserved, its researchers describe it as "looking like a boiled sweet."

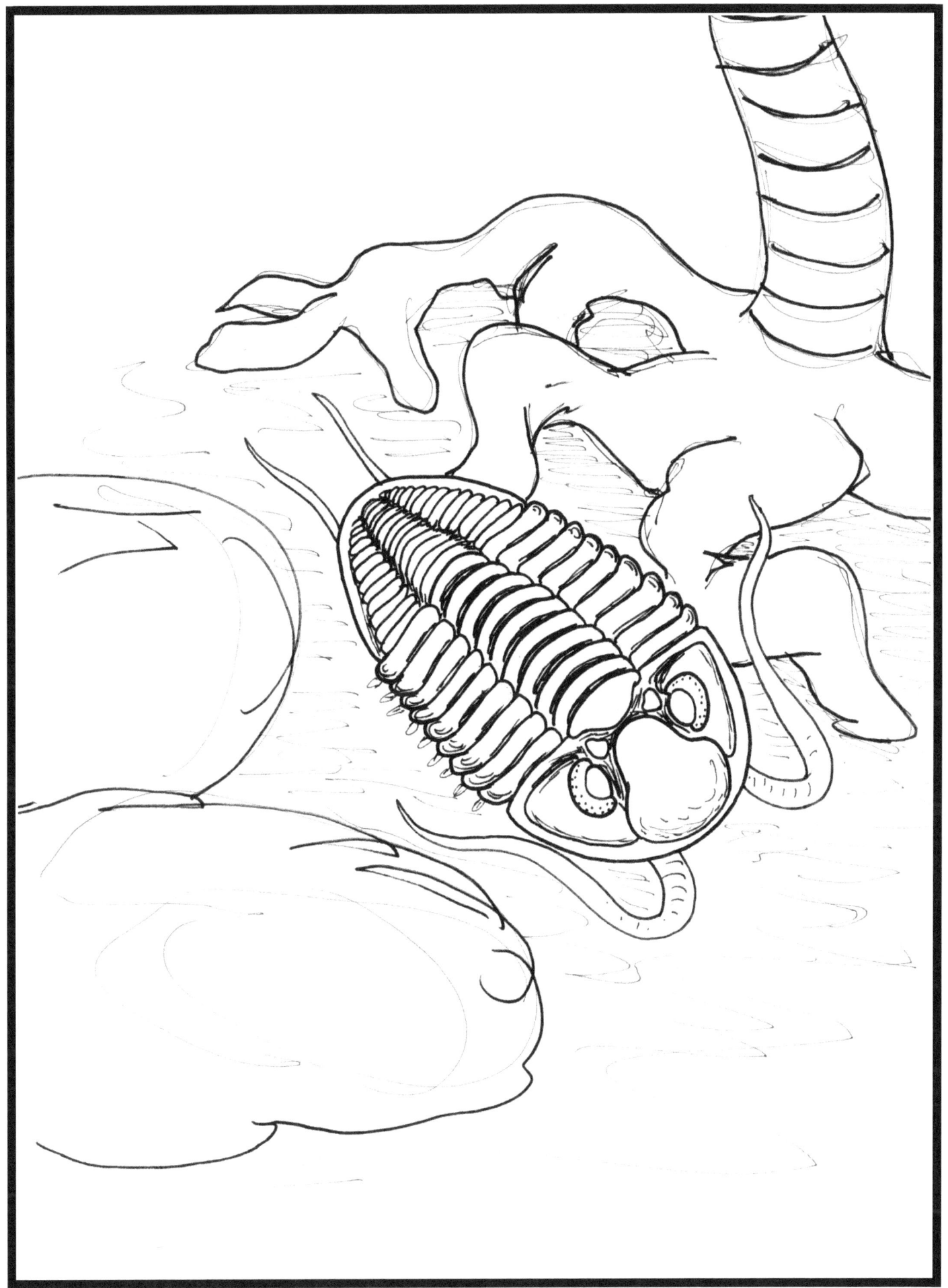

Name

Common Titanhopper

Species	*Gigatitan vulgaris*
Phylum	Arthropoda
Class	Insecta
Order	Titanoptera
Family	Gigatitanidae
Size	Wingspan estimated to be over 28 centimeters
Time Period	Late Triassic, about 235 million years ago
Location	Madygen Formation in Kyrgyzstan
Comments	The Titanhoppers of the extinct insect order Titanoptera lived during the Permian and Triassic periods, and were closely related to modern-day orthopterans such as grasshoppers, katydids and crickets. Most fossils of titanhoppers are of their wings. The Common Titanhopper, *Gigatitan vulgaris*, of Late Triassic Kyrgyzstan, is known from several fossils, including several complete bodies.

These whole-body fossils show an animal similar to a grasshopper or katydid with robust forelegs, and regular-looking hindlegs that did not allow it to hop. The common titanhopper probably preyed on other insects, including primitive orthopterans, which it seized and pinned down with its forelegs similar to the way cone-headed katydids of the genus *Copiphora* capture prey today.

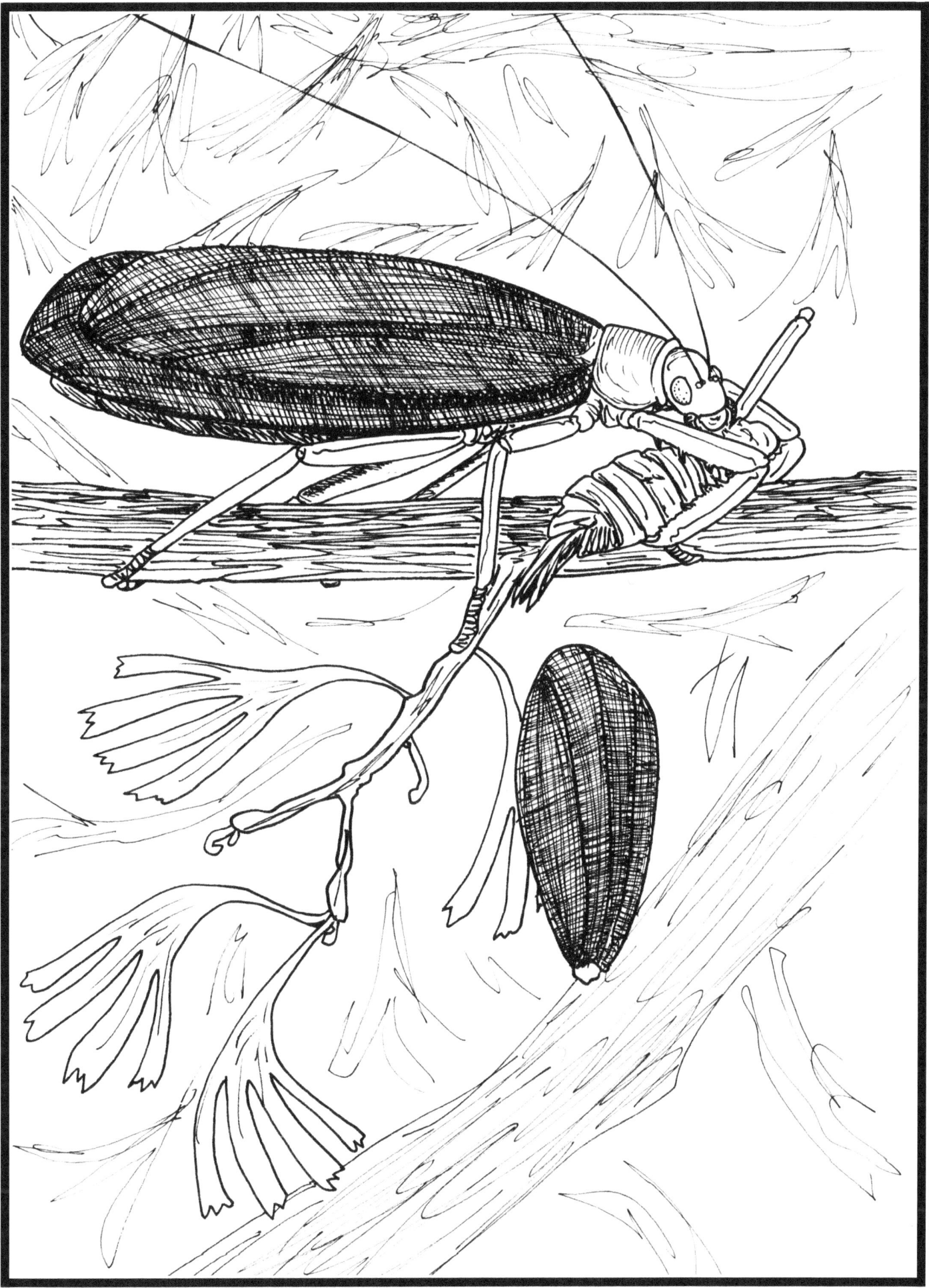

Name   Noble Thunder Lizard

Species	*Brontosaurus excelsus*
Phylum	Chordata
Class	Dinosaurida
Order	Saurischia
Family	Diplodocidae
Size	22 meters long
Time Period	Kimmeridgian Epoch of the Late Jurassic Period, 155 to 152 million years ago
Location	Wyoming and Utah, United States of America
Comments	The Thunder Lizards, especially the Noble Thunder Lizard, have had a long, illustrious and rather sordid relationship with humans (at least the former's fossils). In 1879, Othniel Marsh attempted to get the better of his hated rival, Edward Cope by announcing the discovery of an almost complete skeleton of a giant dinosaur, which he named *Brontosaurus excelsus*, that was missing its skull. In 1903, one Elmer Riggs argued that the material of *Brontosaurus* was too similar to that of the closely related genus *Apatosaurus* to merit being a distinct genus. But, with an evocatively iconic name like "Brontosaurus," the public tends to insist on not getting that memo. In 2015, a group of scientists finally successfully resurrected *Brontosaurus* as a distinct genus. While the public rejoiced, other scientists criticized this as a hair-splitting convention made into a publicity stunt.

The Noble Thunder Lizard was the archetypical sauropod dinosaur, and, was a forest-dweller that, if we assume that it had teeth similar to the related *Diplodocus*, fed by stripping off leaves and conifer needles from tree branches by pulling the branches through their jaws.

Name	Coolerdile
Species	*Koolasuchus cleelandi*
Phylum	Chordata
Class	Amphibia
Order	Temnospondyli
Family	Chigutisauridae
Size	Skull is about 65 centimeters long, estimated to be up to 5 meters long in life.
Time Period	Aptian epoch of the Early Cretaceous, about 120 million years ago
Location	Victoria, Australia
Comments	The Coolerdile, *Koolasuchus cleelandi*, is the youngest known temnospondyl amphibian, a diverse group of terrestrial and aquatic animals that superficially resembled salamanders, lizards and crocodiles (or slimy combinations of all three). Temnospondyls first appeared during the Carboniferous, were most diverse during the Permian, then, after the Permian-Triassic Extinction Event, had another diversification event during the Triassic, and then went into a prolonged decline until only the Coolerdile was left in its frigid stronghold in Antarctic Australia during the Early Cretaceous.

Many temnospondyls, including those of the coolerdile's family, Chigutisauridae, were aquatic predators similar in habit, if not form, to semi-aquatic crocodilians. It is thought that the koolerdile survived as long as it did because it was able to adapt to living in the water systems of partially frozen rift valleys that were too cold for crocodilian competitors.

The coolerdile was a predator that snapped up prey, such as this hapless *Leaellynasaura*, that came within striking range.

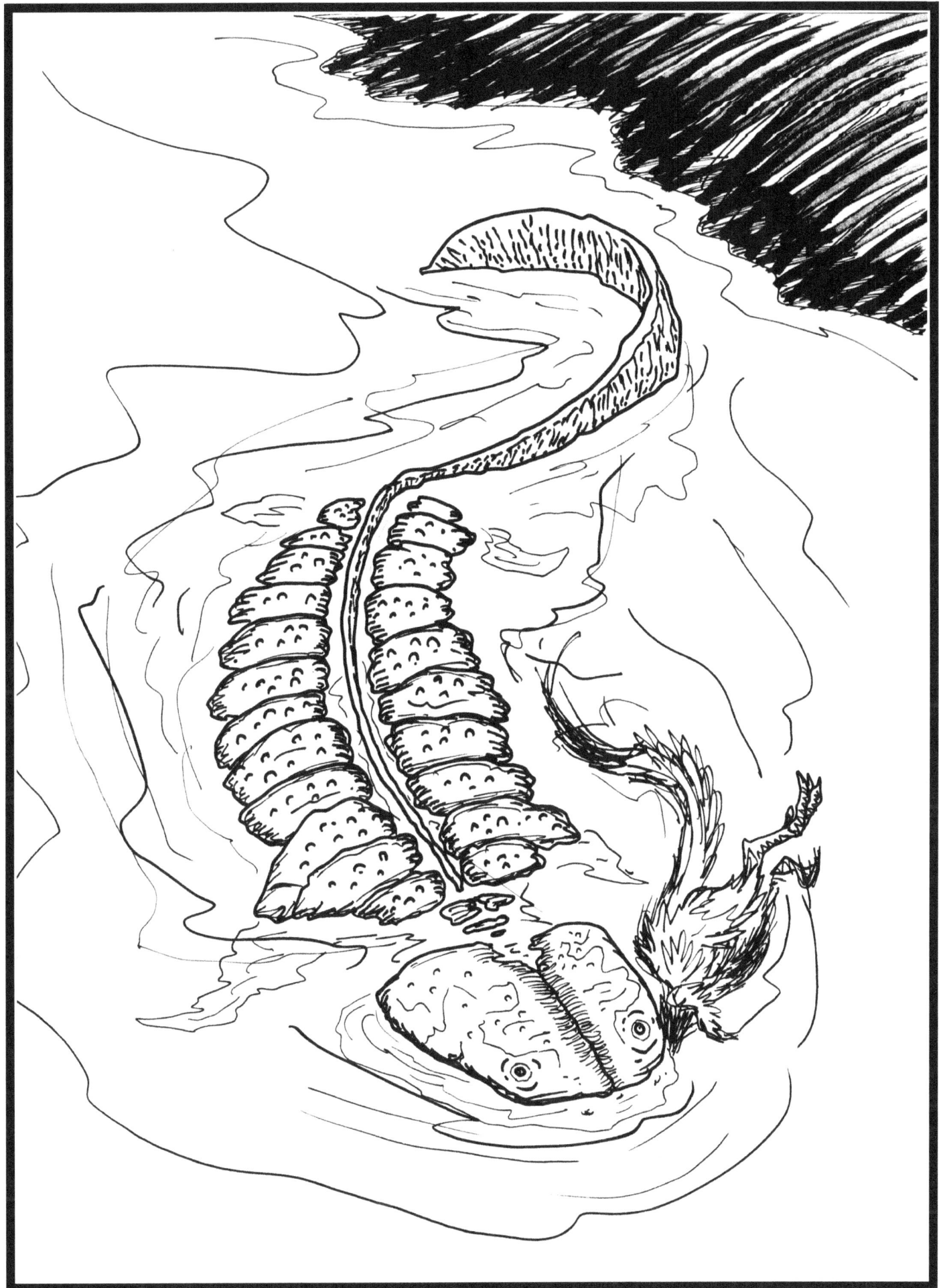

Name	Titanic Boa
Species	*Titanoboa cerrejonensis*
Phylum	Chordata
Class	Reptilia
Order	Squamata
Suborder	Serpentes
Family	Boidae
Size	Estimated to be around 12 meters long
Time Period	Paleocene, about 60 to 58 million years ago
Location	Cerrejón Formation, Department of La Guajira, Colombia
Comments	The Titanic Boa is the largest snake ever known, even larger than the Eocene-aged *Gigantophis* (estimated to be merely 10 meters long). Sets of vertebrae belonging to 28 individuals, as well as cranial bones, are known.

Because of the titanic boa's titanic size, it is popularly thought to have preyed on the many species of crocodilians that lived in the swampy rainforest that is now the Cerrejón coal mines during the Paleocene. However, the biomechanics and chemistry of the fossils suggest that the titanic boa, unlike modern-day boids, hunted and ate fish.

Name	Rulerbeast
Species	*Andrewsarchus mongoliensis*
Phylum	Chordata
Class	Mammalia
Order	? Artiodactyla
Family	*incertae sedis*
Size	Skull 83 centimeters in length, body probably as big or slightly bigger than a Kodiak bear
Time Period	Middle Eocene, 48 to 41 million years ago
Location	Irdin Manha Formation in Inner Mongolia, China
Comments	The Rulerbeast, *Andrewsarchus mongoliensis,* is known from a single skull discovered by Henry Fairfield Osborn Senior from Inner Mongolia, in China, and named in honor of Roy Chapman Andrews. The skull indicates that the original owner was a flesh-eating animal probably bigger than a Kodiak bear or polar bear, or at least bigger than a large water buffalo.

The identity of the rulerbeast has long been debated. Its discoverer, Osborn, argued that it was a mesonychian, a group of carnivorous, hoof-toed ungulates closely related to the cloven-hoofed, or artiodactyl ungulates (including hippos, antelopes and whales). Recent studies suggest that the rulerbeast was not a mesonychian, but an artiodactyl closely related to the hippos, the extinct entelodonts and whales.

Other fossil animals have been misidentified as being either other examples of the rulerbeast, or closely related to it. Below a rulerbeast are three individuals of the mesonychian *Paratriisodon,* on a beach.

Name	Ultimate Titan Hyrax
Species	*Titanohyrax ultimus*
Phylum	Chordata
Class	Mammalia
Order	Hyracoidea
Family	Pliohyracidae
Size	Estimated to be as large as an Indian rhinoceros
Time Period	Late Eocene to Early Oligocene, from 36 to 30 million years ago
Location	Mangrove forests in what is now the Fayum Oasis, Egypt
Comments	Modern-day hyraxes are peculiar herbivorous mammals from Africa and the Middle East, and have been historically mistaken for rabbits. Details of the hyraxes' anatomy show that they are actually related to elephants, dugongs, manatees, tenrecs and the golden mole.

Hyraxes have an extensive fossil record, and several fossil species were fairly large compared to the rabbit-sized species of today. The largest known hyrax is the Ultimate Titan Hyrax, *Titanohyrax ultimus,* from what is now Egypt (related, and slightly smaller species are known from Tunisia), and is estimated to be as big as an Indian rhinoceros. In the picture, a pair of ultimate titan hyraxes are before the related animal *Arsinoitherium*.

Name	Remarkable Snail
Species	*Pseudochloritis insignis*
Phylum	Mollusca
Class	Gastropoda
Order	Stylommatophora
Family	Helicidae
Size	Shell about 2.5 centimeters in diameter
Time Period	Late Langhian to Early Tortonian epochs of the Middle Miocene, 14 to 10 million years ago
Location	Steinheim Basin, in Baden-Württemberg, Southwest Germany
Comments	The Remarkable Snail was originally described as "*Helix insignis*," a close relative of the escargot, *Helix pomatia*. A study published in 2015 showed that it probably not closely related to the escargot; leading the study's authors to remove it from the genus *Helix* and place it in the extinct genus *Pseudochloritis*, and more closely related to the copse snail, *Arianta arbustorum*, instead.
	The remarkable snail is known from several shells collected from a Middle Miocene-aged crater, the Steinheim Basin in Southwest Germany, in what was once a moist forest. Like modern-day helicid snails, the remarkable snail probably ate fungi, and soft or rotting vegetable matter which it rasped away with its radula tongue.

# Name	## Siva's Giraffe
Species	*Sivatherium giganteum*
Phylum	Chordata
Class	Mammalia
Order	Artiodactyla
Family	Giraffidae
Size	About 2.2 meters at the shoulder
Time Period	Pliocene until the early Holocene, from 5 million possibly until 8,000 years ago
Location	India, Pakistan, Iran
Comments	If the Siva's Giraffe, *Sivatherium giganteum*, were seen by people today, they would probably assume it was an odd-looking, overgrown moose. The Siva's giraffe hints at the former diversity within the giraffe family, which had many members that looked vaguely like deer or overly massive antelope.

The skeleton suggests an animal that was 2.2 meters at the shoulders, and 3 meters tall at the uppermost points of the larger pair of ossicones, and weighed over a ton. These measurements would make the Siva's giraffe the largest (but not the tallest!) ruminating artiodactyl ever to have lived.

The living animal was an herbivore that probably browsed on foliage, similar to living giraffes and okapis. Here, the Siva's giraffe is shown with the extinct giant tortoise, *Megalochelys atlas*.

Name	Sardinian Megotter
Species	*Megalenhydris barbaricina*
Phylum	Chordata
Class	Mammalia
Order	Carnivora
Family	Mustelidae
Size	Estimated to be about 2 meters long
Time Period	Late Pleistocene, about 126 thousand years ago
Location	Grotta di Ispinigoli, near Dorgali, Sardinia
Comments	The Sardinian Megotter is the world's largest known otter, and is thought to be larger than the extant Brazilian giant otter, *Pteronura brasiliensis*. The megotter lived in Late Pleistocene Sardinia, and was one of at least four species of otter endemic to the island. All of the Sardinian otters are unrelated to the European otter, *Lutra lutra*, and are, instead, thought to be descended from an extinct otter, *L. simplicidens*, which swam to Sardinia during the Early Pleistocene, before the European otter emigrated out of its ancestral Asia.

There is only one fossil, a partial skeleton, known of the megotter, which remains still embedded in the floor within the cave of Grotta di Ispinigoli. Unlike the situation with the Haoot's fossils in Newfoundland, the rock in which the skeleton is embedded in is simply too hard for scientists to carve away without risking destroying the fossil.

The known portion of the tail shows that the living animal had a large, flattened tail to assist with swimming, and the teeth and jaws show that the animal ate shellfish.

At the top of the picture is the terrestrial *Sardolutra ichnusae*, and in the middle, spying on the megotter's crab lunch, is the semiaquatic *Algolutra majori*.

Name	# Rodriguez Island Giant Day Gecko
Species	*Phelsuma gigas*
Phylum	Chordata
Class	Reptilia
Order	Squamata
Suborder	Sauria
Family	Gekkonidae
Size	Up to 40 centimeters
Time Period	Holocene, last live specimens collected in 1842 AD
Location	Rodriguez Island, in the Indian Ocean
Comments	

The Rodriguez Island Giant Day Gecko, also known as the Giant Day Gecko, and (François) Légaut's Gecko, *Phelsuma gigas*, was the largest known gecko, growing up to 40 centimeters in length, easily surpassing its relative, the Rodriguez Island Day Gecko, or Newton's Gecko, *P. edwardnewtonii*, which grew up to 23 centimeters in length. Like other day geckos, the giant day gecko probably fed on nectar, sweet sap, fruit and insects. It may have also raided birds' nests, as many omnivorous lizards that size are wont to do. Unlike other day geckos, the giant was recorded as being nocturnal in habit. Its somber coloring of charcoal spots on gray to gray-brown, with a yellow belly and throat support this observation. It also allegedly had a pink tongue. By contrast, Newton's gecko, which was diurnal in habit, had a more typical coloration of a bright green back with blue spots and a yellow underside, varying from whitish yellow under the tail, to an eggyolk yellow throat.

Both species are extinct: the last living specimen of the giant day gecko was caught in 1842, while the last Newton's gecko was last seen in 1917. Both are thought to have become extinct due to humans destroying the island's forests, and the introduction of cats and rats that probably preyed on them.

Bibliography

- Anderson, P.S.L.; Westneat, M. (2009). "A biomechanical model of feeding kinematics for Dunkleosteus terrelli (Arthrodira, Placodermi)". *Paleobiology*. **35** (2): 251–269

- Blom, Henning. "New birkeniid anaspid from the Lower Devonian of Scotland and its phylogenetic implications." Palaeontology 55.3 (2012): 641-652.

- Clements, Thomas; Dolocan, Andrei; Martin, Peter; Purnell, Mark A.; Vinther, Jakob; Gabbott, Sarah E. (2016). "The eyes of *Tullimonstrum* reveal a vertebrate affinity". *Nature*.

- Cheke, A. S.; Hume, J. P. (2008). Lost Land of the Dodo: an Ecological History of Mauritius, Réunion & Rodrigues. New Haven and London: T. & A. D. Poyser. ISBN 978-0-7136-6544-4.

- Chen, Feng, Ma, Li, (2003), <u>A New Vetulicolian from the Early Cambrian Chengjiang Fauna in Yunnan of China</u> Acta Geologica Sinica

- Head, J.J; Bloch, J. I; Moreno-Bernal, J. (2013). "Cranial Osteology, Body Size, Systematics and Ecology of the giant Paleocene snake *Titanoboa cerrejonensis*". Vertebrate Paleontology: 140–141.

- Höltke, Olaf; Rasser, Michael w. "*Pseudochloritis insignis*–a peculiar large land-snail from the Miocene of SW Germany: taxonomic status and census of morphologically related forms." Journal of Conchology 42.1 (2015): 1.

- Lamsdell, James C.; Briggs, Derek E. G.; Liu, Huaibao; Witzke, Brian J.; McKay, Robert M. (September 1, 2015). "The oldest described eurypterid: a giant Middle Ordovician (Darriwilian) megalograptid from the Winneshiek Lagerstätte of Iowa". *BMC Evolutionary Biology*. **15**: 169

- Liu, A. G.; Matthews, J. J.; Menon, L. R.; McIlroy, D.; Brasier, M. D. (2014). "Haootia quadriformis n. gen., n. sp., interpreted as a muscular cnidarian impression from the Late Ediacaran period (approx. 560 Ma)". *Proceedings of the Royal Society B: Biological Sciences*. **281** (1793)

- Matsumoto, H. "42. Megalohyrax Andrews and Titanohyrax, gn–A Revision of the Grenera of Hyracoids from the Fayûm, Egypt." *Proceedings of the Zoological Society of London*. Vol. 91. No. 4. Blackwell Publishing Ltd, 1921.

- McCoy, Victoria E.; Saupe, Erin E.; Lamsdell, James C.; Tarhan, Lidya G.; McMahon, Sean; Lidgard, Scott; Mayer, Paul; Whalen, Christopher D.; Soriano, Carmen; Finney, Lydia; Vogt, Stefan; Clark, Elizabeth G.; Anderson, Ross P.; Petermann, Holger; Locatelli, Emma R.; Briggs, Derek E. G. (2016). "The 'Tully monster' is a vertebrate". *Nature*.

- R. A. Fortey and A. P. Heward. 2015. A new, morphologically diverse Permian trilobite fauna from Oman. Acta Palaeontologica Polonica 60:201-216

- Shcherbakov, Dmitry E. "Madygen, Triassic Lagerstätte number one, before and after Sharov." *Alavesia* 2 (2008): 113-124.

- Tschopp, Emanuel, Octávio Mateus, and Roger BJ Benson. "A specimen-level phylogenetic analysis and taxonomic revision of Diplodocidae (Dinosauria,

Sauropoda)." *PeerJ* 3 (2015): e857.

- Willemsen, Gerard F. "Megalenhydris and its relationship to Lutra reconsidered." *Hellenic Journal of Geosciences* 41.8 (2006).
- Warren, Anne, Thomas H. Rich, and Patricia Vickers-Rich. "The last last labyrinthodonts." *PALAEONTOGRAPHICA ABTEILUNG A-STUTTGART*-247 (1997): 1-24.

About the Artist

Stanton F. Fink is a student of Biology and Chinese Medicine, and makes a hobby of drawing monsters and researching flowers, arcane-looking creatures, prehistoric animals, fish, reptiles, birds and the occasional, really grotesque fungal fruiting body.

Stanton grew up and went to school in California and is currently living, drawing, and gardening in Oregon.